# TO DANCE A S

*also by Naomi Wallace*

\*

DRAMA

*Slaughter City*, Faber and Faber (1996)

# To Dance a Stony Field

poems by Naomi Wallace

PETERLOO POETS

First published in 1995
by Peterloo Poets
2 Kelly Gardens, Calstock, Cornwall PL18 9SA, U.K.

© 1995 by Naomi Wallace

All rights reserved. No part of this publication may be reproduced, stored in a retrieval system, or transmitted, in any form or by any means, electronic, mechanical, photocopying, recording or otherwise without the prior permission in writing of the publisher.

A catalogue record for this book is available from the British Library

ISBN 1-871471-54-0

Printed in Great Britain by
Latimer Trend & Company Ltd, Plymouth

## ACKNOWLEDGEMENTS

Grateful acknowledgements are due to the editors of *The American Voice, Bête-Noire, Chelsea, Chicago Review, Hayden's Ferry Review, The Iowa Review, London Magazine, The Massachusetts Review, The Nation, New Statesman & Society, One Meadway, Salmagundi, Stand, ThreePenny Review* and *Verse* in whose pages some of these poems first appeared.

**INVESTMENT**
SOUTH WEST ARTS

*For Bruce*

*Bring all the darkness level with our eyes.*
*It is the poem provides the proper charm,*
*Spelling resistance and the living will,*
*To bring to dance a stony field of fact*
*And set against terror exile or despair*
*The rituals of our humanity.*

— Thomas McGrath

# Contents

## THE LIVING WILL

10 Looking for Karl Marx's Apartment, 28 Dean Street
11 Meat Strike
12 Touching in the Sweatshop
13 The Conquistadores
14 Old Man, Cutting up a Tree and Thinking of Cuba
15 An Execution in the Country
16 Preparing for War
17 Ballad for Gallipoli
18 Framing the Thoughts of a Forefather before the Pequot Battle
19 Kentucky Soldier in the Saudi Desert on the Eve of War
20 Two Sonnets of a Woman Working in the Morgue
21 Killing Time
22 The Divided Garden
23 First Love of a Boy in Amsterdam, 1943
24 Herbert Visiting the Westerbork Transit Camp, Holland
25 Vallejo in the Mines of Quivilca
26 Demonstration in Hyde Park

## THE RITUALS

28 Ode to Blood
29 The Windsurfers
30 The Bath
32 Child Fallen in the Water
33 The Lemons

35 In the Looking Glass
36 Girl Standing Over an Open Grave
37 Ode to a Murdered Child
38 The Terminal
39 The Seam
40 Below the Line
42 The Climb
43 Graft
44 Brighton Cicatrix
45 Travelling the Same Place
46 Snow Angels

*RESISTANCE*

48 The Prisoner
49 The Goat Rattle
50 The Father
51 Prophet Having Seen Jesus Perform a Miracle
52 Valediction
53 Windsurfer near Pozzuoli
54 Notes on an Old Priest's Death
56 Burrasco of Hester Prynne
57 St. Francis and the Hawk
58 The Hunger Madrigal
59 Escape from Paradise, Kentucky
60 Judas in the Fields of Aceldama
61 Young Girl Helping the Prophet Bathe
62 Unrepentant 'Witch' Burned for Adultery in 1503
63 The Devil's Ode

# THE LIVING WILL

## *Looking for Karl Marx's Apartment,*
## *28 Dean Street*

A round, blue plaque on the brick wall, two floors up.
Below it now, though certainly not then, a burly restaurant,
bright lights and food fit for kings. The kind you despised.
Not the food, but the kings. Here you lived with your wife
in poverty. You wouldn't go out on the street for weeks
at a time because you'd pawned your coat and shoes.
Three of your children died up there, behind that glass.
And while Engels worked himself to sickness over
an office desk he despised, just to keep your genius afloat,
history-to-be unfolded in the lungs of your children,
the phlegm so thick it could talk. Did they have, still
children then, nothing to lose but their chains?
No. Not them. Not yet. And while your broken wife wept
on the floor of filth behind you, you stared out the window
at your dream of revolution, the blackened city straining
and shifting under its own dead weight, the working
women and men drifting past your gaze like broken shells.
How long until their day? Inevitable. Inevitable it was,
as was the last abrupt noise your eight year old son Edgar made
when you turned away from that vision, just for a moment,
to see him on the bed, clawing open his own throat for air.

## *Meat Strike*

I haul the split, black slabs of beef, then lay
them on a belt. It isn't my job. The guy whose job
it is stands outside the packhouse, all day,
on strike, uptight, calls me a meat-fucking scab.
At 5 a.m., when we walk in, I look the other way.

I grew up in the city, never touched a cow alive.
Here I touch them in pieces. I stroke them from the inside
out, where they're wet; it's not right. The meat slaps me
hard when I lift it from the hooks. For balance, I lean my head
to the bone. Once I slipped on the guts, took a dive

with my face in it. I could swear that the bloody slab
made a sound, a sneer, like glass dragging on glass.
At 5 p.m. we go home. The man from whom I took this job
until they break the strike, he spits at me. He misses.
He spits again. He misses again. If I could risk this job

I'd ask him if he's heard it, like I did, the meat
talking to him or when his nose is full of blood and his hair
webbed with fat, if he's ever heard it laugh. We're both shit
without money. The Company rolls the coin into the centre
of the strike and we have no choice but to kill for it.

The third time he spits I get it right on the brow.
I still won't look him in the face. I walk through the gate.
If meat laughs, I'd like to tell him, it's because it's how
it's no longer an animal, but flesh turned the wrong way,
turned inside out, as I am, as we both are now.

## Touching in the Sweatshop

Pull the cloth, punch it down, cut three out and trace.
My hands do this thing called work. They are hard-shelled
crabs, scuttling. But not for cover. There is none.
All day my fingers degrade their cheer and grace

among the broadcloths and oil. The boss passes to
and fro, brushes the lint from my neck, tightens
my green apron at the waist. He is good at touching. Gentle.
The way a lover of money handles even the blackest coins.

He whispers in my deaf ear. I say yes because I cannot think
of leaving. There is no other work that my hands can do,
creased in the shape of scissors. When I go home, I am awake
even when I sleep. With my husband, his feet cracked through

from standing all day at the garage, fucking is a necessity.
It's how we talk when any spoken word would be a trespass.
When I daydream, my hands sweep the cloth like water over the keys
of a piano, and I explore the hard, angular bones, as I did as

a young bride, beneath my husband's skin, wiping a drop
of urine from the tip of his sex. But this here. Now. It is not my
dream. When I step away from my body, I want her to stop,
that woman, thickening, bent over her spool like a mantis over a fly.

I can smell her sweat, her sex moving beneath the cloth of her dress.
Sometimes I slide my hand into her blouse and she likes it.
When the boss puts his hand again, like a law between us, we feel less
from his touch and it's one more day that we won't quit.

## *The Conquistadores*

The sand slips like snow through the fingers
of a Spanish army going home. In their helmets
the waves are reflected, breaking against their skulls.
They watch the restless ships chained like bulls
to the sea's floor. Small boats row out
to collect them. Men use their helmets to scoop up
layers of shells while the wind dries their hair,
crusted with sweat and hard weather. Others
rehearse first words for a mother, a brother,
a wife grown old. Each waits his turn for a place
in the row boat while every quarter hour, the sea
pushing at their boots, the whole army steps back.

From this point each of them will go on, though going on
from here can only mean going back — to a city,
perhaps Salamanca, the square burnt dry,
the windows high up, flagged with laundry.
Or to a house in a field — the old stumps are still
in the yard, the fruit pits on the door step, the scraps
of wool under the bed. But after so many years
the quiet ones waiting inside are strange.

## Old Man, Cutting up a Tree and Thinking of Cuba

It cost me three dollars to buy her dentures.
She was just a kid in poverty, and I a bald
American boy with a knack for Caribbean scenes.
She worked down at the wharf, up to her elbows
in squid guts and fish scales, glittering
like charm bracelets on her wrists.
But of course I left, married a nice girl
from Kentucky who had blue-blood to her name.

Sometimes this Cuban wore her dentures
on a string around her neck, to show them off.
Yesterday a storm took down the last oak.
The new blade slips through the soft, green
wood like water. The quake of the chainsaw
shoots through my arms, chest, into my thighs;
when we loved, she put them in a glass of water
next to the bed. She said she liked to feel

my tongue slide across her gums. Never
like that before and never like that again.
I bought her teeth instead of a ring; I believed her
expendable. But it was myself, not her, who was
the whore. Her fingernails. They were black,
sweet, with squid ink. Her mouth tasted of sorghum
and rum. As I stand here now, the rings of this oak tree
read eighty three years old. Last night, just seconds to fall.

## *Execution in the Country*

The sun is above us now, watching.
I scoop the dirt away, handful by handful.
Contras stand over me with guns.
How many times have I done this, prying
open the earth, on a day just like today?
Around this time I might hear the voice of my son
pivoting over the fields, *Come home*,
or in the distance, the figure of my daughter.
With my thumb I could blot her from view,
then make her reappear — such miracles!
Or my wife, floating across the fields towards me,
swinging like a bell over the furrows.
When was the last time I kissed her?
Yesterday? The day before? I must remember.

They force me to lie down in the hole I've dug.
One of the soldiers, the youngest, squats on my stomach.
His chin is like my daughter's. He holds a knife.
For the first time in my life my thighs are heavy
with those of another man — such miracles!
I want to touch him just because he is there above me,
press my mouth to his chest, suck at the heart.
He raises the knife, grits his teeth. I must remember,
I close my eyes and think hard. Suddenly
my thighs swell with a terrible light:
There, by the door! I am sitting there,
yesterday, on the porch. The work is done.
She leans over me and I kiss her open throat.
She tastes like nothing but herself.
She whispers, *Come inside and rest*.


— Nicaragua, 1986

## *Preparing for War*

He drops into the bucket seat, grips the wheel
like the hip bone of his latest lover. She stuck
around after the second hit, his fist sanding
her cheek down to the bone. But it's not the women.
It's how he can't turn it off, that whimper
at the back of his skull, like a rodent caught between

two boards in a wall. He remembers his father
saving him, helping him join up just in time,
before he went sissy at seventeen, trapping katydids,
cataloguing beetles with their hard, black shells
that popped like glass under the pin. He breathes deep,
runs a fuel cloth over his lips and brow.

The other cars, on the inverted line-up, line up.
Their late model frames steam on the blacktop;
their drivers chewing the same grit for luck.
He slams the engine for the warm-up. That roar
of constancy like a cool, black shell over his ears:
how soft her face was on his shoulder, how easily

it broke, like dragging a finger across a web.
As the flag cracks down, the bellow of fans
ruptures the air. And for one moment, before
the rubber makes traction, the vehicle races
at a tremendous speed in one place. And then forward
like a body blasted from one time zone into the next.

— in memory of Paul Barret

## Ballad for Gallipoli

But I wasn't there for England. I was there

because my uncle shot the colt he'd promised me.
Its hooves were split; bleeding, it died in my arms.
The boy to my left because his father struck him

for falling asleep in the furrows while the others planted,

the grass, green flames between his lips.
The boy to my right won't tell us. Maybe he has
a black box inside him, maybe he'll break the lock.

Only once I touched the breast of a woman I loved.

She was my youngest sister. She rose from her bath
in a goblet of light, and with shaking hands
I scraped suds and water from her body.

Her skin was as soft as the breath of a colt.

She smelled like a warm barn, the sour, the song
of the owl. And the bugles sounded above me ...
The bugle sounds for the charge. Not for England

I reach, but for the cup at her mouth.

## *Framing the Thoughts of a Forefather before the Pequot Battle*

This morning is like no other. I halt my horse.
My troops steady behind me. A breeze
cracks like ice against my teeth. The sleeves
of my coat of mail reflect the sky above me
and in my chest the birds fly. The village lies
before us. Quiet. The Braves are gone to battles
twelve miles up river. It was my plan. Clusters
of small children play by the river like flies
on a wound. I count an old man. Two
old women. A Brave, though hardly a man,
both legs gone, drags his tailbone in the dew.
The cruelty of savages, to keep half a man
alive. No man, child or beast
ever died by my hand without at least

a prayer. I pray for my soldiers too, sent
like children to kill children for the piece of land
my horse now freely salutes with excrement.
Myself, it's my fate to be a leader, to take a hand
in this nasty task of clearing the land. The winds
have settled now. In a few, short hours the Braves
will return to this, their sacred home. For some seconds
before the scrambling, begging and slaughtering begins,
before the children drop their sticks and cloth boats,
by surprise, into the water, this crime has no flaw.
Even the silence has blessed the death of these Pequots.
Raising our torches, these crosses made from straw,
I give the signal to move forward. In this sun the lustre
of our armour spills over our breasts like water.

# Kentucky Soldier in the Saudi Desert on the Eve of War

I can't use the latrines, the smell of clorox
and shit, the flies as big as thumbs on the tin walls.
I walk out to the edge of the camp, take a spoon
from my jacket, dig a hole and squat. As a boy
I did the same on the banks of Harrod's creek
while I watched the minnows shoot from rock to rock.
Once my friends and I kidnapped a black kid,
took him down, blindfolded, to the creek.
In a tin can we caught a crayfish, forced the boy's
mouth open with a stick and stuck the critter inside.
The kid screamed so hard we let loose. He spit
the thing out but it left its claw behind on his tongue.
The crayfish lay on the dry rocks, snapping
its one victorious claw in the quiet air

between us; I crushed it under my boot.
I cover my shit with sand. Behaving like a dog,
I feel more like a man. This time it's Arabs. *First
you hate 'em, then you kill 'em.* The Sergeant tells me:
*These are sand-niggers. These are camel-jockeys.*
At night I try not to sleep, but the dreams, they start
in on me again: I am breaking open his jaw, jamming
the crayfish in. But this kid does not scream. This kid
breaks my hold, opens his mouth and the critter
I forced in flies out. Its claw goes for my face,
hangs from my eye like an ornament on a dead tree.
Then I wake up. *First you hate 'em, then you kill 'em.*
Urine pools at my thighs. Under my sheets, the smell
of cold piss is a comfort. Tomorrow we go to war.

# Two Sonnets of a Woman Working in a Morgue

I name her Rika. Her skin is a delicate web.
My finger is an insect that could tear the surface.
This little piggy will wear the 'unknown' tag.
She *went to market* but didn't have a dime.
Will I be left like this on the roadside, a pyre
of old twigs that the sun sets on fire?
A whisper is still in her throat: *A dream is a fly
that fell in the water.* I know, I answer. That's why
I don't dream. Him I name Alexis,
a union man who *stayed home*, on strike,
and got a bullet in the neck for his trouble. His face
is flat and beautiful, like a stone rising out
of the water. I put my finger inside his wound.
He is the first man that I have entered.

I name her Matilda. Her hands are black and thin.
She worked for the assembly line, packing *roast beef*
and heart for the dogs and children of wealthy men.
She rests like someone who's been falling like a leaf
from very high up for years. She drowned
because she *had none* and the bailiffs were mad.
Her mouth is covered in lime: What is the sound
of a shout under water? A lily pad
floats in her dream. Near morning I kiss
them goodnight. Their lips are cold and dark
as plums but not as sweet. We're labour and piss
here below. Our prayer is a fly that doesn't mark
the water. The Lord is not their shepherd at minimum
wage; I am. *All the way home.*

## Killing Time

A spade is buried in one of the graves, wrapped
in the wife's apron with her ball of wax, moustache
scissors and licorice box. The pitchfork hangs
in the arms of what was once a tree or even
a man, the long forks rusted into powder,
fine as a woman's own. But there's no profit.
This farm has been here hundreds of years.
The children are still out back, behind the barn.
They're the ones who can't leave, haven't come in
to supper for years. No one checks to see if
they're still yearning, or merely standing among
the trees, their collars crisp with frost, waiting
for the auctioneers, as the rain, season after season,
fills to the brim their fine young skulls.

## The Divided Garden

Through the war you lived on beetroot
and sucked on stones. You hungered, you said,
like a dog, for the thighs of fleshy
German soldiers. Not to love, but to eat.

Years later you leant over my crib and sang
in Dutch, *sleep, baby, sleep, outside walk
the sheep*: the strife that was yet
to divide us was still safe within.

Once I stopped eating to try and get near
to the place you'd lived in. But there was
no war where I was, no sheep with white
hooves circling the house. I called *Mother*

*Mother*, until you stood beside my bed
as a girl of twelve, an apron full of beetroot,
and stared at me, as one space staring
into another. Once you reached for my face

but then drew back. Once I did the same.
You kept shaking your head like a girl does
with a secret. Then you plunged your hands
into your apron and ate. I cried out in pain

while you kissed me, *hush, hush*. Your lips
were as black and sharp as the hooves of sheep.
You wiped your mouth on my sheet.
And I slept and slept until you were gone.

# First Love of a Boy in Amsterdam, 1943

In the hunger winter, just after they threw me out
of the Party, for stealing apples meant for Jewish friends
in hiding, a surgeon, returning a favour, gave me
some plasma in a bag. A girl was there too, begging,
so I invited her home to share it. We were both seventeen.
Over a flame we fried the blood, Gertje and I.
It was better than eggs. We swooned on the protein richness.
When she kissed me, I giggled. When she kissed me
again I turned away because nothing would rouse my body
from its terrible stupor, not even her strange mouth,
still plump with the infusion of crisp blood. I slipped
my hand into her shirt. The paper rope that held up
my trouser broke apart in her hands. My underbritches
were so filthy that I cursed my own name, envying
the German lads and their fine, white linen
repressing the vigorous flesh that thrived on sweetmeats,
slaughter, and black tea. But Gertje would not give up.
She whispered *Pretend you are nowhere* as she turned me
onto my back. I could smell the sweetness of mould
on her scalp, the lemony sweat from the tufts of hair
under her arms. And then I felt a firing along my spine,
and like a flag her face unfurled inside my head:
I was no where. Yes, no where. And she was with me.


— for Harry de Vries

## *Herbert Visiting the Westerbork Transit Camp, Holland*

Young saplings grow over the graves where they may not
even lie: my mother, so keen on oysters and wool hats,
my father with his large ears, the soft black hair that hid

their openings. My sister's name was Danica, just twelve,
with eyes where one would like to hide old pennies.
But I cannot weep for them as I did as a young man.

Listed among the contented bourgeoisie, I can only rest my hands
on my thickened belly and hang my head. My own children
play on what's left of the rails that went to the camps. I know

they are shouting, but at this distance I only see them jump
and fall. After so many years I still can't keep my mother's words
out of my head: We are Germans; our murderers are German.

Before I escaped, my sister said: They will not kill us; we are
the same family. In the dark her eyebrows, thick as a man's,
were still beautiful, as I could not see the lice.

## Vallejo in the Mines of Quivilca

The *Cholo* breaks out of the mountain rock, a man,
a hunk of stone, blasted, burned, a vein of metal,
a vein of blood pumping across his forehead like a fuse.
His right hand numb, though he still uses it on his wife.
The Company has gone too far, he says, turned us
into dogs and dogs won't dig ore the way a man should.
At home his wife presses the plates onto the table,
slowly, like printing a sign. There's a meeting tonight.
With a shovel she digs up the nail box under the porch.
It's my Uncle's gun, she says, as her husband runs the barrel
over his lips like a salve. This time his wife won't stay home.

As the men walk, their black and soggy lungs swing
like pendulums in their chests. And from way high up,
looking down, the Yankee God of the Tungsten mines
charts the miners' puny trails towards the campfires.

And the God sweats.

## *Demonstration in Hyde Park*

They make their own circle among us, some hundred thousand
well-wishers, do-gooders, out of jobbers, down and outers.
This circle of boys, sons of miners, is out on the street.
One tooth gone, two teeth gone, leather jackets
stitched with nappy pins. This is their day.
They are polite. Their faces white and cold in the rain
that's been soaking us for hours. The Tories want
to shut the mines, to shut their future to follow
their fathers into the earth, to a day of night work,
where compression pumps pump out two hundred
gallons of water every minute, where the silt cuddles
their boots while they titillate the roof to test for a fall,
moving the hydraulic chocks that prop the ceilings, heavy
as cannons, where white slush drips from the underground
roofs until each day is almost like Christmas. But without
the gifts. In this way they earn a pound, two pounds.
How many pounds will British Coal pay for the lungs of one man?
For two lungs? Are they cheaper by the pair?

And the floor of the mine always wants to come up and the roof
to come down, to close the wound wherein the workers
scuttle and crawl, hack and pick. These miner's sons
we call them yobs, rude youth, scraps of British
labour with no place to go. They are cheap to buy.
Their labour is raw and inspired. And best of all, they hate
the stone, the wound that strains to heal each time
they tear it open at the seams. But they are slow to forgive
when lied to. And as their future is mothballed before them,
the grave they've earned the right to is shut down without
notice. And though their fathers are tired, they are not.
Encircled by one hundred thousand of us, these one hundred boys,
like the centre of a flower, grow up quick and straight in the sun.
They are pinning their sleeves back. They are opening
their jackets to the rain. They are gripping pieces of their lives
in their hands: a drill bit, a rubber pipe, a manual on
geological pressures, and they're going to use them.

*THE RITUALS*

## Ode to Blood

We first met, face to face, so to speak, when I was
a girl of twelve. I sat stone-still at breakfast, afraid

to move as my chair filled up with you. *Not the blood
of our Lord*, but old blood from the body: clumps,

bits, the smell of shame, plums and vinegar.
My father strode into the kitchen in his Sunday best,

bristling with light, to herd us outside, quick,
to the car. I refused to budge, buried my face

in a cereal bowl. Alone in the house, I charted
the red thread's journey. *Not the blood of our Fathers,*

but a tickling down my leg as it crossed over a brown,
raised scab on my knee, slipped under the white lace

of my cotton socks and disappeared in my shoe.
Walking out to the yard, I had a different stride.

I sat in the grass and waited, for however long
it would take, this blood with an eye of its own

coming out to look around. Where I sat
the dry grass below me was delirious with drink.

## The Windsurfers

The sea rolls in grey sheets onto the shore.

You are out walking, watching the windsurfers.
The sun burns their sails as they fight for balance,

that grace of compromise between water and wind

There are times I wish you'd never come back to me
as you, but as a boy wearing my face.

Where your flesh ended, mine began. Only our hands

retained their integrity, opening and closing
like lights in a dark room. But now we are

two faces, two places to stand, two sets of blood.

The men drag their boards onto the shore.
Weary, they lie down beside them. The sea has torn

small pieces from their shadows and each time

they return from the waves they are less whole.
One of the youngest, still a boy, is almost transparent.

The sun drills, brilliant, through his chest.

We live and by living we disappear.
Some of the sails fall to the sand as though they were praying.

## The Bath

Your thumb travels her eyelids, slowly,
then over her mouth that is a small wound of fruit.

I watch you bathe her, father and daughter.
On a morning months ago I reached between

my knees and lifted her up from the blood: a flailing
of stunned flesh, an idea full of small

bones, an anonymous child, something of you
and of me, gone. I name her *sleepy fish*,

*peppercorn, fruit pit.* There is a child missing
from your face. That child I hold in my arms.

Sometimes we listen to her weep. In her abandon
we redeem some of our own. As her sorrow insists,

what we need for our own becomes less and less.
As you bathe her, you touch her in a way you've never

touched me. You blow on her neck to dry the damp
folds where my milk, soured, has collected.

She scratches at my breast as she nurses.
We look into each other's gaze: my face, her face,

my face, her face. To go insane or to stay
in the world is a choice between metaphors.

We survive in the small ways: the sweet milk,
the bath, the silly names, your hand on her belly,

my hand. As she grows you call it time passing.
Moving about the room, watching the two of you,

I am also time passing. Cupped in your large hands, her face. When she is clothed you are rewarded:

her smile is a shot of light sprung from a dark hole.

## Child Fallen in the Water

Lying on her back at the bottom of the pond,
    the pain is gone. The pressure of packed cotton
        fills her lungs. Her father's face passes like a pinwheel

over the surface. There is the sound of geese
    and bells, of crickets practising under the mud.
        A ribbon from her dress streams towards the surface.

She reaches but her arms don't reach. The ribbon
    floats above her. The low branches of the trees
        cloud and almost break the surface, spidering

down to claim her. But as the water
    slowly drains of colour, shadows cluster over
        her face. There is the sound of hands clapping

under water, of fish clicking their gills,
    of light turning over. And then the sound
        of something being torn, straight down the centre.

## *The Lemons*

In April they were still tough and green,
strangely proud in the cold sun.

And all around the garden the leaves
conspiring in green on green on green.

By June they turned. The branches sunk
in the wind. The lemons shone with dust.

Some of them fell and rolled down
the hill to the town below us.

Packed tight against the sea's
wind, the town was abandoned now.

The roofs fallen away. The setting sun
cutting its way among the rubble.

At night we'd walk down
the big hill and look back up.

We couldn't see the house where we slept,
where our lives were decided.

But the lemons lit the black hill.
By their marks we found our way home.

The winds and the lemons wedded in August,
and the lemons dropped to the cool ground.

A crisp mist settled on the town.
The rains swarmed in from the sea.

All of it became inseparable in our minds.
Walking down the hill and back

again, your hand would fall
into my hand and stay there.

## *In the Looking Glass*

My face is the landscape of snow where my children
drag their red sleds, their new black mouths
shrieking with joy. There is a rustling of tall pines.
Snow boots puncture the hard snow. The body
that is old now, the body that picks at its grey
hair, I am this body. *There is no rainfall like
your skin*, he said, so I prayed with the women
that beauty would not ransom me to time. But here
I doze now, nodding among my creams and astringents,
picking at the scalp, searching for the grey hair.
Each day a new one and I pluck it out. In my mind
the sleds have turned for home. I follow the path
of their rusted runners into the woods.

## Girl Standing Over an Open Grave

There is the smell of something closed.
The shovelled walls shine with clay as worms

cluster and turn among clear-winged beetles.
The top of her head feels cold.

Her bare feet trace the edge and she notes
the delicate toes, the narrow bone joints

practising under the skin. She dips them
into the air above the grave, balancing.

When she listens hard, she hears a space
filling up space inside her ear.

But the top of her head is hot now,
the sun having passed through the clouds.

Like water the light drains into the grave.
She picks up her shoes to walk home. It's Sunday,

almost dinner: sweet potatoes and gravy thick as tar,
black meats and bread still hot at the centre.

## Ode to a Murdered Child

And I go back to the place I buried her, out behind
the silo, just to the right of the trough. How deep
do I have to dig and how fast? I find the red

blade of a pinwheel, a rubber heel, the silver
bell off a snow cap. What is a root and what
is a bone? The child is a commodity of good soil,

sold by the bag. I put my hand over
your mouth because you broke the law.
My law: obedience to the parent, the school,

the man's head on the coin, raised like a scab.
When I commanded, you would not come.
When I leant down to receive the proper seal,

a repentant kiss from your small lips, you spat.
And spat again from your arsenal of orange pits.
I didn't laugh. That was something I couldn't give up.

Terribly I loved you, but I pushed you to your knees.
I dug the hole. My crime would be so odious
you'd break apart with fear. But you sprung

into the grave with glad impatience, pulled the sod
up to your chin. As you raised your mouth for a kiss,
I shovelled the earth and it fell on your haughty face.

I dig you up but you're not here anymore.
I find only a fruit pit, the blue tooth of a comb,
a snatch of cloth. Sometimes I can still hear you

below me, singing through the dirt in your mouth.
I was a proper citizen; your chaos had no place.
Your resistance was a blade across my face.

## *The Terminal*

Your mouth was once so tender, like a new plant, like
the flesh of a fish. What will we say to each other
after so many years? I am still sentimental.
I have grey hair at my temples. Learning to live
without you, like a potato left in a box, I have grown
new arms, so thin and long and white that each morning
to find them lying at my side is a shock. As it was
a shock to me when you said *You are no longer my child*.
But I am, Mother. I always was. Flesh of my flesh,
I am coming towards you now, through the terminal.
I am an abomination, a vegetable with a heart and a brain,
a bad, bad child with yards of arms trailing
behind me until I reach one of them out, reach one of
them that long way out, to touch the feeding light that is
like a purple flower at the opening of your mouth.

## *The Seam*

Out I dropped. A bloody brick into her bloody arms.
I grew warm and almost human. I had a wooden sled,
a runt pig, a jar of flies. Children don't grow up,
they give up: the breast milk laced with garlic,

the happy whisper, the dry embrace after a bath.
And then a back is turned and then another. How many
footsteps to the door? How many paces to the street?
I peeled off your face with a fish knife

while you slept. I wore it out into my new life.
We don't rot without the ones we love, we live
on without them, shooting forth the phlegm
of our laughter into the face of the past.

See me now, Mother. I am a grown woman
with a face of my own. I turn off the lights
when I tend my own daughter. In the dark
her tiny hands pull at my ears, my chin, searching

for the weak spot in the seam. She fingers the skin
grafts and laughs. I laugh too. We are a conspiracy
that she won't give up; she intends to find me.
Her drool I wear like stitches on my wrist.

Run away, I tell her, holding her tight.
It's not a matter of love, it's a matter of sequence:
the walking away, the voice calling, the slaughter
and the sleep. I turn the light off to tend my daughter.

When she is tall enough to reach the switch, she will
turn it back on. What will she find there, in this chaos
called face? On this cheek where love rested its fingers
like a burning brand, and then went on its way?

## *Below the Line*

1.
My mouth slightly
        open next to my sleeping
                daughter's tiny ear

that fascinates me.
        The form is common
                but below the skin:

the quick, fragmenting blood.
        Her ears among shells
                on a beach, would I

pass them over for more
        intricate shapes?
                This time I won't think

about living any better.
        The city succumbs.
                It is autumn.

The few trees let go. She is
        not sleeping. She is
                sleep. Under the eye

the blood turns like leaves.


2.
The child at my breast
        troubles the vein
                of milk, then asleep.

The tiny face is less
        my own reflection
                than that of a flat

stone under water,
   the vague wash of shadows
      filling its mouth.

If only I could see
   myself here, in
      my own mother's arms,

the bliss still pure,
   not yet exaggerated.
      What else could life yearn

to become after
   this but a slow
      and steady

exaggeration? But then
   the small face like
      a small wave, opens.

— for Nadira

## The Climb

The weight of the new child within me slings me low
and my daughter arrives at the top of the hill before me.
Her tight lungs strain to the tune of crisp air.
Stray roots of the giant tree, thick as a bull's thigh,
surface through the dirt. At our feet, large
brown seeds burst the seams of their shells.
She picks the best among them: the slick ones
that nestle in the palm, the ones that blink the whitest eye.
I stuff my pockets. My daughter fills her wool hat
until it stretches, knobby and grotesque with the shapes
of its fruit. Starting home, I steady myself on her arm
but she shakes me off, zig-zagging down the hill like a sled.
Behind us the branches of the buckeye raise their tent.
The black slabs of bark steam like entrails in the cold air.

## Graft

I stand by your bedside while you sleep, holding in one fist
the courage still left to me. As a child I would plunge my hands
in a bucket of corn for hours, the cool yellow grain bubbling
at my wrists, the smell of rodent and dust. Your hair is like black
leaves on the pillow, a light from outside the window splinters
your forehead that shines like white slate. I don't want to possess you,
but to take on a different form, our mute bodies seizing
an awkward grace, one torso grafting onto the next, the spill
of your breath like grain across my breasts. With haste and happiness,
let me go to hell for this sin; your mouth solders itself to my skull.

## *Brighton Cicatrix*

Your pale skin pivots in the darkness. My gull without feet,
I suck at your relentless breast, push your heart to break

like waves against the steel pilings of the abandoned pier
where the birds hang their dead on slivers of glass that still

bloom from the arcade windows. What is it I want to punish
you for? Is this whine of love I hear, that cuts the water

like a school of fish into ever smaller pieces, only my own?
Under your flesh I search for the feather of the black gull,

the one that has teeth like a dog and feeds from the hip bones
of lovers. With your mouth you draw the night like a splinter

from my blood. Only in the daylight do we find sleep;
our hands breaking under our heads like shells.

## *Travelling the Same Place*

There is a mist here in the mornings.
The gulls hang like fruit in the grey air.

In my mind we are still where I left us —
in the centre of the field. Frozen stalks
of jagged corn line the fence.
At the other end, a river that doesn't move.

I used to dream that inside all things there was
fire — at the back of the brain, in the belly
of the river, in a child's thumb.

I am learning new things here. I've a daughter.
At night I count the short, smooth, infant breaths
pushing in and out like wind through a sieve.

Her cry is abandonment pure. It shudders the night.
Like beauty it finds no comfort. In her sleep
I hear small mutterings of light.

You believed the best stories could only be
built of silence and that the words
were merely noise, trying to break in.

I stopped and I listened but
your silence was twice silence.

That year winter came without a beginning.
Suddenly we were in the middle of it.
The grass was still green under the snow.

## Snow Angels

Five years down the line, your voice
inside my ear like water, where it will trap.
You were my friend, not like a book or a choice
but like the dead weight of an animal asleep in my lap.
As girls we'd strip in the snow, lie down
and let our heads fill with ice. Our buttocks
numb, we'd flail until we lifted from the ground,
our angels below us, faithful in their long socks.
But the sun ate holes through their fledgling wings.
A dog pissed gold on their cottony feet.
I gave you money and the deeds that forfeit brings.
You left with the money. The rule — that love like meat
goes bad in the open air — still stands.
The stink of it is alive on my hands.

*RESISTANCE*

## *The Prisoner*

You squat in a Roman prison, your only light
      the light from insects' wings and the piss trails
of vermin that shine at your feet. How thin
      you must be now. The stone walls are as closed
to your prayers as your disciples' hearts.
      Didn't you know better? Making dead souls walk
was not divine. It was a nasty trick, a slap
      in the Elders' faces. This morning I woke, mouth
locked with blood; you will be crucified.
      Born from the feather of a god, they say, but I
saw a face above me and a mouth of mortal hunger.
      When you were a youngster, I saw you stone a bird
to death with the neighbourhood boys. Tired
      of the game, you blew the dust from its twisted
wing and fingered the severed bone. You wept
      over that body as no human being could ever weep.
I thought the bird must fly from your hands.
      But as a child you knew better, knew right from
wrong; you let what was dead remain that way.

## The Goat Rattle

The earth is warped with rubble, clay and fire.
    I dash from heap to heap seeking my child.
What I fear most is that he'll be whole, unmarked,
    that the other women, caressing the small, green
graves of their infants, will get off their knees,
    unwrap their shrunken scarves and come after me,
to tear me to pieces, as they should, I who was
    cursed with an immortal child. But this dream,
My Lord, you cannot touch. In it I hear my son
    wail, not as wind or fire wails, but as a child
wails, blasted with hunger. I wrench the debris
    from his body and wipe a paste of stone
from his tongue. His feet are crushed: wheat
    under a mill stone. I rejoice; he'll never
walk again. But this is only the dream. My womb
    will bear no more children. It was cursed
the night You dug your hole, planted your seed,
    so my boy would run off to the heavens to be
a god. Like a rag in the sun my child dried up
    on your cross, yet even his death was not
allowed me. He sprang out from the rock, strode
    away, with hardly a word for the rest of us.
In the cave I found his folded rags, black
    and crisp with blood. I beat them on the river's
rocks until they were as clean as boiled fish.
    I wrapped the rags round his infant rattle,
carved from the hip of a goat, and laid them
    in his tomb. Though I stand at his grave, I know
it is empty; I refuse to pray to an empty grave.

## The Father

I was an old man with bunions (they left this
out of the book). They told me *Joseph, go back to your pegs
and boards*. My son not my son. My wife not

my wife. What could I brag when the Elders
came in our midst? I claimed the boy as mine
but to his face I lost face. Once when he was ill

he called *Father, Father*, and I lifted him naked, seething
into my arms. But seeing my face, he struck it
with his tiny fists and said *Not you, not you, but

Him*. I should have wrung his neck right then.
Instead I sniffed his anus for a trace of the God,
but only leather and salt-fish, just like my own.

His lips were strips of slate and his breath so sweet
with myrrh I retched and fled the home. Dressed
as a widow in rags I dogged him 'til he was a man.

It's true that in his light I didn't age.
But when Pilate asked us whom we should release
it was my voice that hurled the name. Not my son,

not my son, but *Barabbas*. When the crowd rose
to my call, victory was mine. Shameful,
shameful it was, but it was mine.

## *Prophet Having Seen Jesus Perform a Miracle*

There were one, two, three fish, five thousand and him
slicing the waves that shone like butter at his feet.
The people chewed, licked and praised. They picked
their gums with fish bones. Children crapped with joy
in the hot sand. That was the story I witnessed.
But I too was born with a vocation, my heart so full
with pilgrimage and blood that as a babe flies swarmed

at my breast to drink. When I became a man, witnessed
my people's hunger, saw them sharpen their stones to kill,
I proclaimed that even the blood of a Roman was sacred.
*Walk with me*, I said, *and you will live in magic*.
I led them out of the village. They had no shoes.
Worms dripped from the nostrils of children.
It was a clear day. I stood before them, just

as he had done. At my feet I lay the tail of a fish,
a strip of leather, softened in goats' blood, a curd
of cheese. I said *Lord, feed your people*. I lifted
my hands to the sky, just as he had done. My arms
were golden with sweat. *Lord*, I said, *multiply
this offering*. And we were patient, hour after hour.
The sun was so hot on our head that our hair cracked

and broke like twigs in our hands. Two hungry
children were the last of them to curse me and return
to the village. I begged them to kill me. I gave the boy
a knife and lay prostrate at his feet. The girl leant over me
and laughed, a white paste of saliva ringing her lips.
A strand of her hair fell across my brow. To this day
I believe she was an angel, though not one of his.

## *Valediction*

A pigeon fell in front of us on the path to your sister's grave.
One of its wings was severed from the bone. I said I wanted
to kill the bird. I was twelve then, older than you, but you said
*Leave it be. It's Christ's bird.* So we kept walking while behind us
the one good wing beat against the stone. I was your only friend.

Your infant sister died by your father's boot. Her round belly,
where you squashed your ear to hear the fizzy bubbles, turned blue.
Your mother ran to and fro in the yard, the rain shredding her dress.
You said you could see your sister, under the dirt, the light trapped
in her mouth, her hair still alive, sprouting from the skull like grass.

> *But that's not you that's your sister*
> *buried there don't poke at the grave*
> *with a stick no she isn't thirsty I*
> *don't know what sound you're talking*
> *about you can't tickle the dead leave*
> *those feathers where you found them.*

When we walked home the pigeon was gone. Maybe a gardener.
Maybe a dog. How did you know it was Christ's bird? You said
*By how the eyes close.* Your father lived to be an old man.
Your mother walked out of the yard and never came back.
You said she was Christ's bird and when you leant over her coffin

she spat a stone into your hand, *For luck*, she said. You lifted
her blouse and stuffed her with white feathers. *For luck*, you said.
After the funeral we stood out in the clear, green rain, two girls,
holding hands. I wanted to ask you but I couldn't. You knew
so you said *She told me we were going to live as long as a stone lives.*

— for Claudia Bischoff

## *Windsurfer near Pozzuoli*

The sea is white under the sun. It was just like that,
you think, just like Christ's flesh, as you swing up
onto the board. You are twenty-one, half-naked,
in love, as you bolt into the wind. Closing your eyes,

legs slightly bent, you open your mouth wide and the wind
cleans it out. Your brown ankles flash like stones.
You are arrogance, brilliance, your torso planted firmly
on the board as though you were born there, upright

from the sea, bloodied not by women but by foam.
The water snaps against your thighs. You think
of her mouth finding you in those places,
how you held her down, forced her to breathe

through your mouth. How you conquered
and by conquering found balance. But it's good
to believe in God. You feel the sun preying on your back,
the water springing to your neck. You say to hell

with the shoreline. To hell with the little crowd
mumbling on the beach among the shells. To hell
with the lone figure of your mother running down the beach
waving her arms to bring you back into the shallows.

She opens her mouth, like a fish, you think, and calls your name.
You ignore her. Your palms are raw from holding the pole.
Just like him, just like him, until a wave explodes
against your chest and you fall, crown first, into the sea.

## Notes on an Old Priest's Death

Last night he dreamt he found her asleep inside
a giant shell and he lay down beside her, his head
on her sleeve. His breath drained, sand
into the warm air. Next to his, her body stirred

like leaves under water. Sitting now in the yard
of the small church by the harbour, he waits
for his last day. No one comes to ask how he is
feeling, no basket of bread wrapped in cloth, no

chicken blackened in the fire, no prayer
from *their* lips. He thinks he might die
with less of their notice than that accorded
a small tree fallen over the road and then

moved aside: *He should not throw her out once
he has let her in but it is fifty-two years ago
and she has come to his door saying "Save me,
Father," as though saying her own name.*

*She is naked but for a belt on her waist.
Her flesh stinks of whiskey and salt and sailor.
Because he is young and in need of a mortal
sin to live his life repenting for, he lets her in.*

*Later in the night, over a candle, he burns the skin
from his hands, then throws her out. In the morning
the grass below his window is crushed
as though an animal had slept there.*

He stands up to go back inside. He has sat
too long in the sun. His head feels light
as though inside his skull a bird is opening
its wings. On the morning of the day of his death

he gets out of bed, sweating heavily. The room
smells of blackberries and eel. He opens the door.
*Come back in*, he says. *Come back in.*
The wind slides like sand over the roof. In the yard

the new sun cracks like ice through the branches.
No one is there but she is there, the belt ringing
her naked waist. He kneels before her in the grass,
reciting a prayer not meant for the Lord.

## *Burrasco of Hester Prynne*

In the woods my horse goes lame and I dismount.
He finds us. He leans over to lift the hoof. The light
wraps like a collar 'round his neck. He is a Minister.

There is a stone in the hoof; it will heal. My husband,
two years absent, is perhaps at the bottom of the sea
with an urchin nesting at the back of his throat.

But this Minister, his hair as black as — yes, it's true —
as black as sin, is what I want now, to take his thin face
in my hands, suck on his mouth as one might god's.

But I can't move. I watch his hand slide up, then down,
the flank of my horse. He holds the animal as I remount
and remarks that the hem of my robe is damp from the moss.

As I take the reins his breath passes across the back
of my hand. As I turn my horse to go, it is then that he calls
my first name: *Hester*. And then again: *Hester*. I can not

spur my horse forward. He lifts my skirt and his mouth
opens onto my knee and it is a mouth like the wound
in the side of Christ, our Lord: I put my fingers inside it.

## St. Francis and the Hawk

A shark's eye, among the leaves, that won't
come like others come: sparrow hawk.
I spit in my hand for you to drink. I butt
my face against the tree. Other birds flock
at my breast with their curse-driven wings
as the Lord insists. You are impudent, starving,
I tear off my nail; my bald finger sings
its blood and should tempt you. The villagers are lying;
I'm not a man, so how can I live among men?
The stink of public loneliness drives me mad
with its dreams of cock and dung. Come, descend
to my crown and pick from my scalp your food.
Pick away at the brain, this last wealth of men
until my mind is as empty as my God's again.

# The Hunger Madrigal

Lying here, I know he's afraid, though blest,
to touch me: there is nothing more intimate
than death. He runs his hand over my chest
as if trailing fingers in water and I'm pleased.
When he begs *eat, eat*, it is the call of a jay
in my head and doesn't harm. In mirrors I notice
my bones display under the skin like jewelry
under glass. This body is my masterpiece:
probing, craving, caressing, with rare deceit.
Yet in my dreams I am all flesh. My hair
hangs over my face like strips of meat.
I am not *in* this dream, I am it. Like a prayer,
I force him to accept my ever stricter poise.
To punish him I make love without making a noise.

## *Escape from Paradise, Kentucky*

They came from King's Island, their chins sticky with soda,
fingers webbed with cotton candy, herding onto the bus home.
The children shoved and prodded into the seats that would kill
or chuck them like dice, burning into the safe air.
The truck hit the bus head on, precisely, as though years ago

it had already taken aim. The bus exploded to a stop.
The faces that would live stared for a moment into the faces
that wouldn't. There was a silence then, one that would torment
those who survived long afterwards: the silence of bodies falling
from high up, tilting this way and that like porpoises in the air.

Before the screaming began, before the clawing and trampling
to get out of the flaming bus, with an inhuman grace the children
nodded to the plan; not with their brittle, quick knowledge
but with their spines, which had already begun to blaze
inside their backs like good veins of coal.

## *Judas in the Fields of Aceldama*

But the field was mine. I paid for it with silver
and a curse to him who promised to deliver us.
I paid with my soul that He lifted from my body
like a pea from the dirt. I took the money
as a gift for making him grand. He was but a boy
until they hung him, a boy with skinny legs

and on the cross he wiggled like a pegged bird
until the spirit left him. But he got his due
for what I'd done. Some say the crown of thorns
was clawed from his head by a monstrous bird
and carried away. So I made the deal, bought
the land, dug the holes and scraped the seeds

from my pockets. They split and fouled in my hands.
I scooped up a palmful of dirt and looked into it:
there is your face, He said, leaning down over me
with his furious breath. And far up on the hill
I heard the other one cry out and I knew what
he meant and I cursed him for the immortality

he would lay across my name. Because I too
was forsaken. The wind burned and spit like fat
across my Aceldama, and though I didn't move an inch
from where I stood, I watched my body walk out towards
a tree on the edge of the field and hang itself.
And I wept there, and I was alone, at my body's feet.

## Young Girl Helping the Prophet Bathe

I shouldn't be here, watching you in the bath.
Your shoulders stung brown by the sun, your black
hair like ashes over your skin. I can smell
your mouth even from this distance, your breath
breaks the way a stone breaks the water.
When I want you like this I can hear the blood

in my mouth, circling to get out. I can't
have you. Not tomorrow. Not one day.
In my dream I kiss the bones under your skin.
My breath slides its blade through your hair.
But already you are watching the water drain out

through your feet. First your knees, then calves,
then ankles appear from the receding water.
If I could stop this now, keep us here forever;
with the knots of your spine turning under my hand,
the water sucking at your heels, the white stone
of the bath swelling under your thighs.

## *Unrepentant 'Witch' Burned for Adultery in 1503*

In the face of happiness. I spit in the face of happiness.
They want the truth. I give it to them like a cup of air.
Singing for my life, I sang their lie, that crackle and hiss,
that pardon from the paradise of flesh, but it did no good.
They'll have me dead. Circling me, they take off their hats.
A small child carries the torch and lights the sticks.
I can smell the slippers begin to burn on my feet.
In my head your breast, glazed with sweat, meets
my breast. The light curls like a silkworm in your hair.
Where are the rains He promised us, to drench us, to rot
the caps from our knees? No. I won't repent by His law.
Your kiss is a leaf that falls from high up: I must catch it.
Your tongue is so plump with blood, so cold it covers
my skin with frost as the fire, like scissors, opens my dress.

## The Devil's Ode

More radiant than God himself, I was. My wings
were hung with pinecones and the strung ribs
of a calf were my crown. But I fell in love
with a mortal; not to recreate myself but to spy
out love in the tampered flesh, and she was not
afraid of me. Hardly glancing at the manifest

of my wings, she threw me handfuls of corn
from the field where she worked and turned her back.
Not as an angel should behave then, but as a swine,
I got down on all fours and feasted. If I were
patient she would toss me a glance. For this I wept,
over the gutted stalks, the shameless husks, the bodies

of glutinous wasps, swooning to the earth, drunk
on fermenting corn. Only when my shrunken wings
lay rotting in the field did she let me kiss her.
But that was enough. It gave me a power more terrible
than God's and my heart screeched like a goat
in flames. Because of this, because I knelt

before a mortal, He cast me out, shredded my wings,
set me alight. Burning like a pine forest I fell
through the sky into the earth. Though I am cursed,
I snicker under the dirt. From this place I can
reach up and fondle the dumb, blistered steps
of his mortals, the women and men who stagger

the earth to die. He can touch only the tops
of their heads that pray, cold, through the brain.
Down here I tend the roots of the corn stalks
that will blast through the crust to the sun.
Through the dirt I kiss the bottoms of their feet,
their very souls, without breaking their strides.